CONTENTS

Music Leader

Lyrics and Motions

Lyric and Guitar Chord Charts

Snowball Mountain Challenge:
Find Your Strength in God

	Bible Story	Lift Lessons	Music	Crafts
Session 1	Joseph Interprets Dreams (Genesis 40:1–41:45)	I can share my gifts!	• Snowball Mountain Challenge • Philippians 4:13 • I've Got a Gift • Snowball Mountain Day	• Mosaic Snowflake • Kaleidoscope • Chalet • Fan
Session 2	Esther Shows Courage (Esther 3:7–8:8)	I can be brave!	• I've Got a Gift • Snowball Mountain Challenge • C-O-U-R-A-G-E • Snowball Mountain Day	• Watercolor Mountain • Seal Paper Doll • Twirl Toy
Session 3	The Widow's Offering (Mark 12:41-44)	I can give my all!	• Philippians 4:13 • Anything But You • Supersized • Snowball Mountain Challenge	• Air Clay Snow Challenger • Upcycle Prayer Box • Coin Charm
Session 4	Jesus Prays in the Garden (Matthew 26:36-46)	I can pray!	• Philippians 4:13 • The Journey • This Is What I Pray • Jump Up! Walk a Little	• Diamond Art Suncatcher • Flip Book • Ribbon Paper Wreath
Session 5	Peter and John at the Temple (Acts 3:1-10)	I can hope!	• Snowball Mountain Challenge • C-O-U-R-A-G-E • Jump Up! Walk a Little • The Journey	• Challenge Medal • Cocoa Mug Frame • Scroll Paper Art • Tissue Paper Stars

Includes Music station helps PLUS lyrics, and motions for ALL VBS songs!

Music Leader

Cokesbury Editorial/Design Team

Sarah Gregory .... Development Editor
Kaitlyn Depoister .... Production Editor
Keitha Vincent .... Production and Design Manager
Micah Kandros .... Logo Design

Cokesbury Administrative Team

Brian K. Milford .... President and Publisher
Marjorie M. Pon .... Associate Publisher and Editor, Church School Publications
Scott Spradley .... Director and Editor, VBS
Heather Wegenka .... Business Manager
Karla Taylor .... Marketing Manager

Consulting and Production Team

Andy Wilson .... Songwriter and Producer
B4Entertainment .... Video Producer
Adelicia Company .... Video Producer

Thank you to our consultant team! VBS 2026 Contributors, Reviewers, Testers, and Focus Group Members:

Our Team:
Keitha Vincent, Matt Allison (Development Assistance), Megan Ranjit, Selena Cunningham, Jonathan Higdon, Sarah Gregory, Scott Spradley, Karla Taylor (Marketing), Hank Hayes (Marketing), Dakota Rimmer (Marketing), Heather Wegenka (Business Manager)

Test Churches:
A&M United Methodist Church, College Station, TX; Connell Memorial United Methodist Church, Goodlettsville, TN; Heritage Presbyterian Church, Mason, OH; Zion Lutheran Church, Tamaqua, PA

Reviewers and Focus Group Members:
Michael Haspe, Tamaqua, PA; Amy Jo Alspaugh, Charlotte, NC; Rebecca Dyck, Chapel Hill, NC; Mallory Anderson, Lebanon, TN; Susie Faas, Mason, OH; Jenn Huff, Bloomington, IN; Susan Midkiff, Show Low, AZ; Salley Millsap, Murfreesboro, TN; Caitlin Bookwalter, Ormond Beach, FL; Lauren Bedevian; Houston, TX; Amy Perry, Burlington, VT; Becky Betz, Sugarland, TX; Kelsey Sledge, Cookeville, TN; David Barton, Goodlettsville, TN; Alayna Barton Peters, Goodlettsville, TN; Ashlea Barton, Goodlettsville, TN; Savannah Salas, College Station, TX; Mimi Sanders, Tucker, GA; Becci Benson, Enterprise, AL; Laurie Hembree, League City, TX; Lisa Kutinac, League City, TX; Andrea Jenkins, Virginia Beach, VA; Jan Russell, Minneapolis; MN, Amy Takahashi, Raleigh, NC; Brooke Wong, White House, TN; Charlotte Trafton, Austin, TX; Hannah Pratt, Murfreesboro, TN; Jayne´Kirk, Hurricane, WV; Jamie Muller, Tucker, GA; Kacie Jumper, Temple, TX; Lori Grasty, Elkhart, IN; Liz Greenban, Lake Arrowhead, CA; Laura Stinnett, Humble, TX; Sue Nieman, Lambertville, MI; Tiffany McClure, John's Creek, GA; Tiffany Barton, Goodlettsville, TN

Cokesbury VBS 2026
Snowball Mountain Challenge
Find Your Strength in God
Music Leader

ISBN: 9781791037567

Published by Abingdon Press, 810 12th Avenue South, Nashville, TN 37203. This leader book is part of Cokesbury's ***Snowball Mountain Challenge***

If you have questions or comments about using this resource, call 800-672-1789, a toll-free service available Monday through Friday from 8:00 to 4:00 Central Time. Calls at other times are recorded for response the next working day.

Two convenient ways to order in the U.S.: call 800-672-1789 or visit CokesburyVBS.com.

To place an order in Canada, call 800-265-6397 or email info@afcanada.com.

I can do all things through him who strengthens me. (Philippians 4:13, NRSV)

Science	Recreation	Snacks	Notes
• Straw Lift • Homemade Gummy Candy	• Laundry Basket Bobsled Race • Freezing Dreams Tag • Icy Mountain Motto Challenge	• Snowflakes • Snowflake Cupcakes • I Can Share My Gifts!	
• Instant Freeze • Blubber Glove	• Bible Verse Snowball Fling • Winter Clothes Race • Snow Queen/King Contest	• Snow-Drizzled Treats • Donut Snowman • I Can Be Brave!	
• Ball Bearing Ice • Notebook Tension	• Widow's Offering Hockey • Challengers' Slalom Race • Footprints in the Snow	• Hot Chocolate Mix • Snowman Pudding • I Can Give My All!	
• Coding Journey • Instant Snow	• Carry-for-Others Sled • Ice Skating Spin • Crawl and Waddle	• Snow Cream Dip • Ollie • I Can Pray!	
• Snowshoe Mountain Challenge • Soda Explosion	• Ski Lift Limbo • Cross-Country Skiing • Gold or Silver? NO!	• Snow-Covered Popcorn • Winter Sports • I Can Hope!	

Equipping Your Music Station

Welcome to *Snowball Mountain Challenge VBS*
Get your VBS started as Music Leader by following these simple tips:

- Attend all Snowball Mountain Challenge leader training sessions to learn about the program and how your station fits into the overall message.

- Be ready! Listen to the **Snowball Mountain Challenge Complete Music CD** in its entirety, and practice the hand and body motions with your team.

- Choreography instruction videos for all 10 VBS music videos are now available both on the Cokesbury VBS YouTube Channel and on our Free Resources tab at CokesburyVBS.com. *Instructional videos were created for dancers in music videos and are provided at no additional charge as a courtesy. In some cases, lyrics may differ slightly from official lyrics or spoken directions may differ from printed directions.*

- Note that motions directions are written from the leader (mirror) perspective and may include the following abbreviations:

L (left)	R (right)
LH (left hand)	RH (right hand)
ASL (American Sign Language)	

- If you will be hosting Challengers with differing abilities, please consult the "VBS for Participants with Differing Abilities" resource at CokesburyVBS.com to learn how to include all students and encourage them to participate at their own comfort levels.

- Use the **Student Take-Home CD** to familiarize your Challengers with their VBS music. Hand these out in advance at registration or at your Community Celebration! If your families don't have a CD player, they'll be able to follow the link on the disc face of each CD to download MP3 files to play on their devices. Please do not share these links publicly as the music is copyright protected.

- Purchase music videos and MP3 audio tracks songs at CokesburyVBS.com.

***Directions are written from the perspective of "on stage" leaders facing Challengers.

To easily download Choreography videos, an Assembly Time countdown, Bible backgrounds, and more visit: https://rebrand.ly/SMCfreechoreocdvideos or scan the code below.

Snowball Mountain Challenge (Theme Song)

Intro

Step, touch, and clap to the beat

Can you feel it in your heart?
Can you feel it in your soul?
Are you ready for the challenge?
Do you wanna go?

Sway side to side and swipe hands down arms/chest
Twinkle fingers down on "soul"
Point RH, Point LH, Point RH, Point LH
March in place

Pre-Chorus
As we move
Into the great unknown,
God provides
Strength we've never known. This is a

Pretend to snowboard down a hill R foot forward
Pretend to snowboard down a hill L foot forward
Fingers raining down like blessings
Make strong arms, moving up from waist

Chorus
Snowball (Snowball) Mountain (Mountain)
Challenge! This is a
Snow! (Snow!) Ball! (Ball!) Moun! (Moun!) Tain!
(Tain!) Challenge!
No matter what the future brings,
With Jesus we can do all things
Snowball (Snowball) Mountain (Mountain)
Challenge!
Let's go, let's go, let's go!

Pretend to ice skate side to side
Pretend to ski R to L
Pretend to ice skate side to side
Pretend to ski R to L
Swipe hands across body to indicate "no"
Point to God, jump up and down with fist in the air
Pretend to ice skate side to side
Pretend to ski R to L
Make "come here" motions with hands and fist pump on the last "go"

The snow is deep,
The path is steep
But I've got you and
You've got me and
We've got Jesus!

Sway side to side and swipe hands down arms/chest
Twinkle fingers down on "soul"
Point RH, Point LH, Point RH, Point LH
March in place
Point up to God

Repeat Pre-Chorus
Repeat Chorus

Bridge
Climb, climb, climb up Snowball Mountain, then we
Slide, slide, slide on down that hill. We gonna
Climb, climb, climb up Snowball Mountain, then we
Slide, slide, slide on down that hill

Quickly climb in place
Slide L with arms out, slide R with arms out
Quickly climb in place
Slide L with arms out, slide R with arms out

Repeat Pre-Chorus
Repeat Chorus

Words and Music by: Andy Wilson, Cross Kid Nation

Philippians 4:13

Lyrics	Motions
Snap your fingers like this, everybody come on	*Snap fingers to the beat*
(Let me tell you, let me tell you 'bout Jesus)	
Clap your hands like this, everybody come on	*Clap hands to the beat*
(Let me tell you, let me tell you 'bout Jesus)	
Chorus	
I can do all things	*Walk 4x L, pointing to self*
Through him who gives me strength	*Walk 4x R, pointing to God, strong arms on "strength"*
Through him who gives me strength	*Walk 4x L, pointing to God, strong arms on "strength"*
I can do all things!	*Point to self, burst arms up and open*
I can do all things	*Walk 4x L, pointing to self*
Through him who gives me strength	*Walk 4x R, pointing to God, strong arms on "strength"*
Through him who gives me strength	*Walk 4x L, pointing to God, strong arms on "strength"*
I can do all things,	*Point to self, burst arms up and open*
Philippians four thirteen	*Open Bible hands, cross arms to self*
Post Chorus	
If you ask me what Jesus can do (All things)	*Point forward and rock side to side, open arms "all"*
He never fails; his promises are true	*Swipe hands "no", point up to God*
If you ask what Jesus helps me do (All things)	*Point forward and rock side to side, open arms "all"*
Whatever I may face, I know he'll see me through	*Move head side to side, add looking hands on forehead*
Tag	
When I'm fearful, he makes me brave,	*Lean, step back, palms facing out*
Gives me courage on the way	*Alternating strong arms*
When I'm tearful, he hears me pray	*Hands to face like "tears"*
Gives me hope in all I face	*Alternating strong arms double time*
Won't matter if I win or lose,	*Move arms and body "Matrix" style*
I know he will see me through	*Repeat in the opposite direction*
Repeat Chorus	
Repeat Post-Chorus	
Repeat Tag	
'Cause I can do all things	*Walk 4x L, pointing to self*
Through him who gives me strength	*Walk 4x R, pointing to God, strong arms on "strength"*
Through him who gives me strength	*Walk 4x L, pointing to God, strong arms on "strength"*
I can do all things!	*Point to self, burst arms up and open*
I can do all things	*Walk 4x L, pointing to self*
Through him who gives me strength	*Walk 4x R, pointing to God, strong arms on "strength"*
Through him who gives me strength	*Walk 4x L, pointing to God, strong arms on "strength"*
I can do all things,	*Point to self, burst arms up and open*
Philippians four thirteen	*Open Bible hands, cross arms to self*

Words and Music by: Andy Wilson, Crosskid Nation

I've Got a Gift

Lyrics	Motions
Heart full of fear,	*Clap hands 4x down by L leg*
But I've made my decision	*Clap hands 4x down by R leg*
I'll share the gifts	*Clap hands 4x down by L leg*
You give to make a difference	*Clap hands 4x down by R leg*
God, fill me with strength,	*Clap hands 4x up to L*
You are all I need	*Clap hands 4x up to R*
The time has come, the moment's here,	*Point to each wrist, point down*
I know that you're near, so	*Hug yourself*
Chorus	
I've got a gift I'm gonna give,	*Freestyle dance*
I've got a gift my God has given,	
I've got a gift, and I'll share it with the world	
I've got a fire deep inside,	
Can't stop it, I won't even try	
I've got a gift, and I'll share it with the world	*Scoop arms 4x on share, circle arms up on world*
Heart full of hope,	*Clap hands 4x down by L leg*
Sometimes I can't believe it	*Clap hands 4x down by R leg*
You choose someone	*Clap hands 4x down by L leg*
Like me to make a difference	*Clap hands 4x down by R leg*
My whole heart is yours,	*Clap hands 4x up to L*
You're the one I'm living for	*Clap hands 4x up to R*
The time has come, the moment's here,	*Point to each wrist, point down*
I know that you're near, so	*Hug yourself*
Repeat Chorus	
In everything I say and do,	*Step together step, point to the corner 2X L, then step*
Make me more and more like you	*together step, point to the corner 2X R*
God, fill me with your strength,	*Step together step, point to the corner 2X L, then step*
Help me use the gifts you give	*together step, point to the corner 2X R*
(Repeat)	*Hug yourself and nod on "help"*
Repeat Chorus	
I've got a gift I'm gonna give,	*Freestyle dance*
I've got a gift my God has given,	
I've got a gift, and I'll share it with the world	*Scoop arms 4x on share, circle arms up on world*

Words and Music by: Andy Wilson, Crosskid Nation

C-O-U-R-A-G-E

La, la, la, la, la, la, La, la, la, la, la, la, La, la, la, la, la	*Sway side to side*
When I feel surrounded,	*Step out/in LR, arms reach out and in around self*
When I feel afraid,	*Step out/in LR, hug yourself*
When I feel discouraged,	*Step out/in LR, hold head in hands*
Help is on the way	*Step out/in LR, straight arms up to God*
No matter where, I know you're there	*Step out/in LR, shake hands out*
With courage for each day	*Step out/in LR, prayer hands*
Your peace guards my heart and	*Step out/in LR, hands over heart or point to heart*
Your love makes me brave	*Step out/in LR, strong arms*
Pre-Chorus	
Oh-oh-oh-oh-oh I know I'm not alone	*2 steps L with circle arms above head, then repeat R*
Oh-oh-oh-oh-oh your love makes me strong	*2 steps L with circle arms above head, strong arms R*
Greater is the one living in me,	*Step L, step R with rolling arms 2x*
You give me all that I need, and you fill me with	*Step L, step R with rolling arms 2x*
Chorus	
C-O-U-R-A-G-E, C-O-U-R-A-G-E, It comes from you and flows through me, That C-O-U-R-A-G-E	*4-step turn around self with elbows out and crossing over chest, point to God on "you" and self on "me"*
La, la, la, la, la, la, La, la, la, la, la, la, La, la, la, la, la	*Sway side to side*
When my heart is hurting,	*Step out/in LR, arms reach out and in around self*
When I'm feeling low,	*Step out/in LR, hug yourself*
You're the one I run to,	*Step out/in LR, hold head in hands*
You're my source of hope	*Step out/in LR, straight arms up to God*
No matter where, I know you're there	*Step out/in LR, shake hands out*
With courage for each day	*Step out/in LR, prayer hands*
Your peace guards my heart and	*Step out/in LR, hands over heart or point to heart*
Your love makes me brave	*Step out/in LR, strong arms*
Repeat Pre-Chorus *Repeat Chorus*	
Bridge	
You make me brave! I know you'll make a way! When it seems there's no way! You make me brave!	*Step front L and point up R, step front R and point up L 4 times, strong arms on "brave"*
You make me brave! I know you'll make a way! When it seems there's no way!	*Step front L and point up R, step front R and point up L 4 times, strong arms on "brave"*
You make me B-R-A-V-E BRAVE!	*Fist pump 5x, strong arms on "brave"*
Repeat Pre-Chorus *Repeat Chorus 2X*	

Words and Music by: Andy Wilson, Crosskid Nation

Supersized

Intro	*Use fingers to countdown 4-3-2-1*
If one plus one is two, and two plus two is four,	*Point R finger to L elbow, alternating to the beat 4x (add numbers if desired) while marching*
Then how'd the widow's gift add up to so much more?	*arms out with palms facing up, then "raise the roof" while marching*
When we follow Jesus, it can't be denied,	*Point R finger to L elbow, alternating to the beat 4x*
In God's eyes, what we give is supersized!	*R hand to eyes to look L, then repeat to R, pulse hands starting up, moving down to your sides*
Pre-Chorus	
So put your hands in the air, everybody dance	*March L 4x, waving arms in air L to R*
Doesn't matter who's watchin', go ahead and take a chance	*Step together step L 2x with hand above eyes, then repeat R, pointing finger 2x*
If you're giving all you've got, you're doing it right	*March L 4x, waving arms in air L to R*
In God's eyes, what we give is supersized!	*Look L, Look R,, pulse circle arms down*
Chorus	
Let's go oh-oh-oh-oh-oh-oh	*Knees in, knees out with hands around mouth*
That's right oh-oh-oh-oh-oh-oh	*Fist pump jump on "right"* *Knees in, knees out with hands around mouth*
Rah oh-oh-oh-oh-oh-oh	*Fist pump jump on "rah," look L, look R,*
In God's eyes, what we give is supersized!	*Pulse circle arms down*
You see, it doesn't add up, one plus one's not three,	*Point R finger to L elbow, alternating to the beat 4x (add numbers if desired) while marching*
But that's what Jesus does with generosity	*arms out with palms facing up, then "raise the roof" while marching*
He looks at the heart and he sees what's deep inside	*Point R finger to L elbow, alternating to the beat 4x*
In God's eyes, what we give is supersized!	*R hand to eyes to look L, then repeat to R, pulse hands starting up, moving down to your sides*
Repeat Pre-Chorus *Repeat Chorus*	
We give our time and our talents and our money too	*Point to wrists, rub fingers together to show "money" while marching*
We give it all with joy because it comes from you	*arms out with palms facing up, then "raise the roof" while marching Point R finger to L elbow, alternating to the beat 4x*
You give all we need because you always provide.	
In God's eyes, what we give is supersized!	*R hand to eyes to look L, then repeat to R, pulse hands starting up, moving down to your sides*

Repeat Pre-Chorus
Repeat Chorus

Words and Music by: Andy Wilson, Crosskid Nation

This is What I Pray

I pray in the morning,	*Prayer hands together*
Thankful for each day	*Move arms up with palms facing out*
I pray in the evening,	*Prayer hands together*
For the many ways	*Move arms down with palms facing out*
Pre-Chorus	
You give me grace,	*L arm scoop out in front of body*
Fill me with peace,	*R arm scoop out in front of body*
Here is what I say,	*Use hands to make talking movements from mouth*
this is what I pray:	*Prayer hands together*
Chorus	
Not my will, but yours be done	*Swipe hands in front of body, point to God*
I am yours	*Bring hands down together and place over heart*
Make my life an offering	*Praise hands moving up*
For your glory	*Circle arms going down 2X*
God, I want to honor you in all I do and say,	*Arms out in front of body, open arms to sides*
I need you every day,	*Rolling hands up and in towards face with palms open*
This is what I pray	*Prayer hands together*
Oo-oo-oo-oo, Oo-oo-oo	*Sway*
I pray all the time 'cause	*Prayer hands together*
I know you're listening	*L hand to L ear, R hand to R ear*
I don't have to worry	*Hug yourself and shake head "no"*
Because you're here with me	*Nod head "yes"*
Repeat Pre-Chorus	
Repeat Chorus 2X	
Oh, I need you every day,	*Rolling hands up and in towards face with palms open*
This is what I pray	*Prayer hands together*
This is what I pray	*Prayer hands together*

Words and Music by: Andy Wilson, Crosskid Nation

Jump Up! Walk a Little

What I hope for can't be bought,
But you give me all you've got
What you offer is what I need,
Got the power to get me on my feet so

Sway side to side, swing arms out then cross over body 3X

Sway side to side, point to feet

Pre-Chorus
I put all my hope in you,
I put all my hope in you, Jesus oh
I know there is nothing you can't do,
I was helpless, I was weak,
You set me on my feet so I can

Step L 2X, point to self, step R 2x, point to God
Step L 2X, point to self, step R 2x, point to God
Step L 2X, point to self, step R 2x, point to God
Bend over at waist and flop like a rag doll
Point to feet

Chorus
Jump up! Walk a little little
Jump up! Walk a little more (repeat)

Jump with arm point up 2x, walk fast L
Jump with arm point up 2x, walk fast R

Can't believe it, you blow my mind
All I long for, you provide
What you offer is what I need,
Got the power to get me on my feet so

Sway side to side, swing arms out then cross over body 3X

Sway side to side, point to feet

Repeat Pre-Chorus
Repeat Chorus
Repeat Pre-Chorus

Jump up! Walk a little little
Jump up! Walk a little more (4x)

Jump with arm point up 2x, walk fast L
Jump with arm point up 2x, walk fast R

Words and Music by: Andy Wilson, Crosskid Nation

Anything but You (Preschool)

Lyrics	Motions
Nothing can compare	*Wave arms in front of body*
To all that you have done for me	*Cross arms over heart*
I'm so thankful and my heart	*Point to God*
Can't help but sing	*Bring pointed hands down in front of body*
Pre-Chorus	
You're the love that never fails,	*Wave arms in front of body*
A savior and friend,	*Cross arms over heart*
One who's always there	*Point to God*
And fills me with his strength	*Bring pointed hands down in front of body* *Bring strong arms up on "strength"*
Chorus	
I don't want anything but you	*Cross hands in front of body "no", point to God*
I don't want anything but you	*Cross hands in front of body "no", point to God*
I don't want anything but, anything but	*Cross hands in front of body "no" 4x*
You oh you oh you oh you are	*Point to God 4x*
Everything to me	*Circle arms up, cross arms over heart*
Yes, you are everything to me	*Circle arms up, cross arms over heart*
I don't want anything but,	*Cross hands in front of body "no" 4x*
Anything but You	*Point to God*
La, la, la, la, la, La, la, la, la, la,	*Skip around*
When I'm feeling down	*Wave arms in front of body*
You are there to pick me up	*Cross arms over heart*
You provide the strength	*Point to God*
That helps me when I'm stuck	*Bring pointed hands down in front of body, stand still in place on "stuck"*
Repeat Pre-Chorus	
Repeat Chorus	
La, la, la, la, la, La, la, la, la, la,	*Skip around*
Repeat Chorus	

Words and Music by: Andy Wilson, Crosskid Nation

The Journey (Snowball Mountain)

Lyrics	Motions
Way up high on Snowball Mountain	*Raise L arm up, close fist and bring to side*
Far above the tallest trees	*Raise R arm up, close fist and bring to side*
All the beauty of creation	*Raise L arm up, close fist and bring to side*
On display for all to see	*Raise R arm up, close fist and bring to side*
Chorus	
Who knows where the journey goes?	*Arms out in front of body then open 2x*
But we know who is with us every	*Cross arms over self*
Step along the way	*Walk in place*
In God we find strength for all time	*Point to God, bring arms up to strong arms*
We need your strength to help us carry on	*Cross arms over self, walk in place*
Every challenge we will face and	*Raise L arm up, close fist and bring to side*
Every obstacle we find	*Raise R arm up, close fist and bring to side*
We rely on God to guide us	*Raise L arm up, close fist and bring to side*
Trusting that God will provide	*Raise R arm up, close fist and bring to side*
Repeat Chorus	
We can't stay on Snowball Mountain	*Raise L arm up, close fist and bring to side*
There's a world in need of hope	*Raise R arm up, close fist and bring to side*
So, we go in God's great power	*Raise L arm up, close fist and bring to side*
To share the love that Jesus shows	*Raise R arm up, close fist and bring to side*
Who knows where the journey goes	*Arms out in front of body then open 2x*
But we know who's with us every	*Cross arms over self*
Step along the way	*Walk in place*
In God we find strength for all time	*Point to God, bring arms up to strong arms*
We need your strength to help us carry on	*Cross arms over self, walk in place*
We're trusting God will lead us safely home	*Point arms up to God, then point down to ground*
From Snowball Mountain	*Arms out to cross 1 at a time, then bring together above head to make a mountain*

Snowball Mountain Day

Intro

March in place 2 8-counts

It's cold outside but it's
Warm in our hearts and all
Our friends are here and
The party's getting started
We clap our hands and we
Sing and shout
(ah, wooooo!)
Jesus you're the reason for a

Step 4x L cross arms over body and shiver "brrrr"
Step 4x R rub hands together
Step 4x L point both hands
Step 4x R "raise the roof"
Step 4x L clap hands
Step 4x R hold microphone "karaoke walk"
Step 4x L cup hands around mouth
Center Alternating L and R hands pointing up

Chorus
Snowball mountain day
It's gonna be a snowball mountain day
Everybody dance and celebrate
It's gonna be a snowball mountain day

Step L roll hands, step R roll hands
Step L throw snowballs, step R throw snowballs 2X
Freestyle dance 8 counts
Step L roll hands, step R roll hands
Step L throw snowballs, step R throw snowballs

We look around at all
That you have done for us
You changed our minds and
You change our hearts and
So, we clap our hands and we
We sing and shout (ah, wooooo!)
Jesus, you're the reason for a

Step 4x L hands to forehead "searching"
Step 4x R both arms out palms up
Step 4x L point to self
Step 4x R hands to heart
Step 4x L clap hands
Step 4x R hold microphone "karaoke walk"
Step 4x L cup hands around mouth
Center Alternating L and R hands pointing up

Repeat Chorus

Bridge
Everybody do the snowball slide
Now take it from the left back to the right
Wiggle just a little from side to side
Everybody do the snowball slide
Everybody do the snowball slide
Now take it from the left back to the right
Wiggle just a little from side to side
Everybody do the snowball slide

Big step slide R, big step slide L
Slide R, Slide L
Lean and wiggle R, lean and wiggle L
Shuffle feet slide R, shuffle feet slide L
Big step slide R, big step slide L
Slide R, Slide L
Lean and wiggle R, lean and wiggle L
Shuffle feet slide R, shuffle feet slide L

We clap our hands and we
We sing and shout (ah, wooooo!)
Jesus You're the reason for a

Step 4x L clap hands
Step 4x R hold microphone "karaoke walk"
Step 4x L cup hands around mouth
Center Alternating L and R hands pointing up

Repeat Chorus
Repeat Bridge

Words and Music by: Andy Wilson, Crosskid Nation

Snowball Mountain Challenge (Theme Song)

Intro: E E A/E B/E F#m/E E

E
Can you feel it in your heart?
A/E B/E F#m/E E
Can you feel it in your soul?
E
Are you ready for the challenge?
A/E B/E F#m/E E
Do you wanna go?

Pre-Chorus
A B
As we move
G#m7 A
Into the great unknown,
A B
God provides
G#m7 A
Strength we've never known. This is a

Chorus
E A B
Snowball (Snowball) Mountain (Mountain) Challenge! This is a
E A B
Snow! (Snow!) Ball! (Ball!) Moun! (Moun!) Tain! (Tain!) Challenge!
C#m A B E
No matter what the future brings,
C#m A B
With Jesus we can do all things
E A B
Snowball (Snowball) Mountain (Mountain) Challenge!
E
Let's go, let's go, let's go!

E
The snow is deep,
A/E B/E F#m/E E
The path is steep
E
But I've got you and
A/E B/E F#m/E E
You've got me and
F#m7 E
We've got Jesus!

Repeat Pre-Chorus
Repeat Chorus

Bridge
E F#m G F#m
Climb, climb, climb up Snowball Mountain, then we
E E6 E
Slide, slide, slide on down that hill. We gonna
E F#m G F#m
Climb, climb, climb up Snowball Mountain, then we
E E6 E
Slide, slide, slide on down that hill. We gonna
Repeat Pre-Chorus
Repeat Chorus

Words and Music by: Andy Wilson, Crosskid Nation

Philippians 4:13

Ebm7 Abm7
Snap your fingers like this, everybody come on (Let me tell you, let me tell you 'bout Jesus)
Ebm7 Abm7
Clap your hands like this, everybody come on (Let me tell you, let me tell you 'bout Jesus)

Chorus
Ebm7 Abm7
I can do all things through him who gives me strength
Ebm7 Abm7 Bb7
Through him who gives me strength I can do all things!
Ebm7 Abm7
I can do all things through him who gives me strength
Ebm7 Abm7 Bb7
Through him who gives me strength. I can do all things! Philippians four thirteen

Post Chorus
Ebm7 Ab7(9)
If you ask me what Jesus can do (All things)
Ebm7 Abm7
He never fails; his promises are true
Ebm7 Ab7(9)
If you ask what Jesus helps me do (All things)
Ebm7 Abm7 Bbm7 B7 Daug
Whatever I may face, I know he'll see me through

Tag
Ebm7
When I'm fearful, he makes me brave, gives me courage on the way
Ebm7 Bb/Eb
When I'm tearful, he hears me pray, gives me hope in all I face
B7 Bbm7
Won't matter if I win or lose,
B7 Bbaug
I know he will see me through

Repeat Chorus
Repeat Post-Chorus
Repeat Tag

Ebm7 Abm7
I can do all things through him who gives me strength
Ebm7 Abm7 Bb7
Through him who gives me strength I can do all things!
Ebm7 Abm7
I can do all things through him who gives me strength
Ebm7 Abm7 Bb7
Through him who gives me strength. I can do all things!

Words and Music by: Andy Wilson, Crosskid Nation

I've Got a Gift

Intro: Bbm7 Dbsus2 F#sus2 Absus4

Bbm7 Dbsus2 F#sus2 Absus4
Heart full of fear, but I've made my decision
Bbm7 Dbsus2 F#sus2 Absus4
I'll share the gifts you give to make a difference
Bbm7 Dbsus2 F#sus2 Absus4
God, fill me with strength, you are all I need
Bbm7 Dbsus2
The time has come, the moment's here, I know that you're near, so

Chorus
F#7sus2 Absus4 Db Bbm7 F#sus2
I've got a gift I'm gonna give, I've got a gift my God has given,
Absus4 Ab/Db Bbm7(11)
I've got a gift, and I'll share it with the world
F#7sus2 Absus4 Db Bbm7 F#sus2
I've got a fire deep inside, can't stop it, I won't even try
Absus4 Ab/Db Bbm7(11)
I've got a gift, and I'll share it with the world

Bbm7 Dbsus2 F#sus2 Absus4

Bbm7 Dbsus2 F#sus2 Absus4
Heart full of hope, sometimes I can't believe it
Bbm7Dbsus2 F#sus2 Absus4
You choose someone like me to make a difference
Bbm7 Dbsus2 F#sus2 Absus4
My whole heart is yours, you're the one I'm living for
Bbm7 Dbsus2
The time has come, the moment's here, I know that you're near, so

Repeat Chorus

F#sus2 Absus4 Bbm7(11) Db9 x2

F#sus2 Absus4 Bbm7(11) Db9
In everything I say and do, make me more and more like you
F#sus2 Absus4 Bbm7(11) Db9
God, fill me with your strength, help me use the gifts you give
Repeat

Repeat Chorus
Absus4 Db Bbm7 F#sus2
I've got a gift I'm gonna give, I've got a gift my God has given,
Absus4
I've got a gift, and I'll share it with the world

Words and Music by: Andy Wilson, Crosskid Nation

C-O-U-R-A-G-E

Fm C7
La, la, la, la, la, la, La, la, la, la, la, la, La, la, la, la, la

Fm Eb/F Fm
When I feel surrounded, when I feel afraid,
Fm Eb/F Fm
When I feel discouraged, help is on the way
Fm Eb/F Fm
No matter where, I know you're there with courage for each day
Fm Eb/F Fm
Your peace guards my heart and your love makes me brave

Pre-Chorus
Db Ab Eb Fm
Oh-oh-oh-oh-oh I know I'm not alone
Db Ab Eb Fm
Oh-oh-oh-oh-oh your love makes me strong
Ab Eb Fm
Greater is the one living in me,
Db C7
You give me all that I need, and you fill me with

Chorus
Fm
C-O-U-R-A-G-E, C-O-U-R-A-G-E,
Fm
It comes from you and flows through me,
Fm
That C-O-U-R-A-G-E

Fm C7
La, la, la, la, la, la, La, la, la, la, la, la, La, la, la, la, la

Fm Eb/F Fm
When my heart is hurting, when I'm feeling low,
Fm Eb/F Fm
You're the one I run to, you're my source of hope
Fm Eb/F Fm
No matter where, I know you're there with courage for each day
Fm Eb/F Fm
Your peace guards my heart and your love makes me brave

Repeat Pre-Chorus
Repeat Chorus

Bridge
Fm
You make me brave! I know you'll make a way!
Fm Eb Fm
When it seems there's no way! You make me brave!

Fm
You make me brave! I know you'll make a way!
Fm Eb
When it seems there's no way! You make me B-R-A-V-E BRAVE!

Repeat Pre-Chorus
Repeat Chorus 2X

Words and Music by: Andy Wilson, Crosskid Nation

Supersized

Intro Eb5 Db/F Gb Ab Bb7

Eb5 Ab7
If one plus one is two, and two plus two is four,
Eb5 Ab7
Then how'd the widow's gift add up to so much more?
Eb5 Ab7 Eb5 Db/F Gb Ab Bb7
When we follow Jesus, it can't be denied. In God's eyes, what we give is supersized!

Pre-Chorus
Eb5
So put your hands in the air, everybody dance
Db/Eb Eb5
Doesn't matter who's watchin', go ahead and take a chance
Eb5 Eb5 Db/F Gb Ab Bb7
If you're giving all you've got, you're doing it right. In God's eyes, what we give is supersized!

Chorus
Eb5 Ab7 Eb5 Ab7
Let's go oh-oh-oh-oh-oh-oh That's right oh-oh-oh-oh-oh-oh
Eb5 Ab7
Rah oh-oh-oh-oh-oh-oh
Eb5 Db/F Gb Ab Bb7
In God's eyes, what we give is supersized!

Eb5 Ab7
You see, it doesn't add up, one plus one's not three,
Eb5 Ab7
But that's what Jesus does with generosity
Eb5 Ab7 Eb5 Db/F Gb Ab Bb7
He looks at the heart and he sees what's deep inside. In God's eyes, what we give is supersized!

Repeat Pre-Chorus
Repeat Chorus

Eb5 Ab7
We give our time and our talents and our money too
Eb5 Ab7
We give it all with joy because it comes from you
Eb5 Ab7 Eb5 Db/F Gb Ab Bb7
You give all we need because you always provide. In God's eyes, what we give is supersized!

Repeat Pre-Chorus
Repeat Chorus

Words and Music by: Andy Wilson, Crosskid Nation

This is What I Pray

Intro: Bb Cm Gm Eb x2

```
Bb              Cm  Gm                    Eb
I pray in the morning, thankful for each day
Bb              Cm  Gm                    Eb
I pray in the evening, for the many ways
```

Pre-Chorus

```
Bb          Cm      Gm    Eb
You give me grace, fill me with peace,
Bb              Cm      Gm    Eb
Here is what I say, this is what I pray:
```

Chorus

```
F                   Gm              Eb          Bb
Not my will, but yours be done I am yours
F                   Gm          F/A    Bb  Eb   Bb
Make my life an offering For your glory
F                   Gm                  Eb          Bb
God, I want to honor you in all I do and say,
F                   Gm      Bb/D
I need you every day,
Eb                  Bb
This is what I pray
```

```
Bb          Cm          Gm          Eb
Oo-oo-oo-oo, Oo-oo-oo
```

```
Bb              Cm          Gm              Eb
I pray all the time 'cause I know you're listening
Bb              Cm  Gm                      Eb
I don't have to worry  because you're here with me
```

Repeat Pre-Chorus
Repeat Chorus 2X

```
F                   Gm              Bb/D
Oh, I need you every day,
Eb                  Bb
This is what I pray
Eb                  Bb
This is what I pray
```

Words and Music by: Andy Wilson, Crosskid Nation

Jump Up! Walk a Little

Intro Dm G Bb A7

Dm G Bb A7
What I hope for can't be bought,
Dm G Bb A7
But you give me all you've got
Dm G Bb A7
What you offer is what I need,
Dm G Bb A7
Got the power to get me on my feet so

Pre-Chorus
Bb C F C/E Dm C
I put all my hope in you,
Bb C F C/E Dm C
I put all my hope in you, Jesus oh
Bb C F C/E Dm
I know there is nothing you can't do,
C Bb Bb6
I was helpless, I was weak,
A7
You set me on my feet so I can

Chorus
Dm G
Jump up! Walk a little little
Bb A7
Jump up! Walk a little more (repeat)

Dm G Bb A7
Can't believe it, you blow my mind
Dm G Bb A7
All I long for, you provide
Dm G Bb A7
What you offer is what I need
Dm G Bb A7
Got the power to get me on my feet so

Repeat Pre-Chorus
Repeat Chorus
Repeat Pre-Chorus
Repeat Chorus (x4)

Words and Music by: Andy Wilson, Crosskid Nation

Anything but You (Preschool)

Intro B F# E F# (x2)

B E F# B B F#/A#
Nothing can compare to all that you have done for me
G#m E C#m F#
I'm so thankful and my heart, can't help but sing

Pre-Chorus
B E
You're the love that never fails,
F# B B F#/A#
A savior and friend,
G#m E
One who's always there
C#m F#
And fills me with his strength

Chorus
E F# F#/D# G#m
I don't want anything but you, I don't want anything but you
C#m F#
I don't want anything but, anything but
B C#m B/D#
You oh you oh you oh you are
E F# F#/D# G#m
Everything to me yes, you are everything to me
C#m
I don't want anything but,
F# B
Anything but you

B F# E F# B F# E F#
La, la, la, la, la, La, la, la, la, la,

B E F# B B F#/A#
When I'm feeling down you are there to pick me up
G#m E C#m F#
You provide the strength that helps me when I'm stuck

Repeat Pre-Chorus
Repeat Chorus

B F# E F# B F# E F#
La, la, la, la, la, La, la, la, la, la,

Repeat Chorus

Words and Music by: Andy Wilson, Crosskid Nation

The Journey (Snowball Mountain)

Intro F F Bb C (x2)

F Bb C F Bb C
Way up high on Snowball Mountain far above the tallest trees
F Bb CBb C F
All the beauty of creation on display for all to see

Chorus
Bb F/A Gm C/E F
Who knows where the journey goes?
Gm F/A Bb C
But we know who is with us every step along the way
Bb F/A Gm C/E F Gm F/A C
In God we find strength for all time we need your strength to help us carry on

F Bb C F Bb C
Every challenge we will face and every obstacle we find
F Bb C Bb C F
We rely on God to guide us trusting that God will provide

Repeat Chorus

F Bb C F Bb C
We can't stay on Snowball Mountain there's a world in need of hope
F Bb C Bb C F
So, we go in God's great power to share the love that Jesus shows

Bb F/A Gm C/E F
Who knows where the journey goes?
Gm F/A Bb C
But we know who is with us every step along the way
Bb F/A Gm C/E F Gm F/A C
In God we find strength for all time we need your strength to help us carry on
Gm F/A C
We're trusting God will lead us safely home
F
From Snowball Mountain

Words and Music by: Andy Wilson, Crosskid Nation

Snowball Mountain Day

Intro Esus2 A6sus2 F#m Bsus4

```
E                                    A                                  F#m
It's cold outside but it's warm in our hearts and all
F#m                                              B
Our friends are here. The party's getting started
E                                      A                                F#m
We clap our hands and we, we sing and shout (ah, wooooo!)
B
Jesus you're the reason for a
```

Chorus

```
E                               A
Snowball mountain day
                    F#m                           B
It's gonna be a snowball mountain day
              E                     A
Everybody dance and celebrate
                    F#m                      B
It's gonna be a snowball mountain day
```

```
E                                    A
We look around at all that you have done for us
F#m                                          Bsus4
You changed our minds and you change our hearts and
E                                              A                                F#m
We clap our hands and we, we sing and shout (ah, wooooo!)
B
Jesus, you're the reason for a
```

Repeat Chorus

Bridge

```
E                                              E
Everybody do the snowball slide now take it from the left back to the right
E                                                E
Wiggle just a little from side to side everybody do the snowball slide
E                                                          E
Everybody do the snowball slide. Take it from the left back to the right
E                                                E
Wiggle just a little from side to side everybody do the snowball slide
```

```
E
We clap our hands and we
A                         F#m
We sing and shout (ah, wooooo!)
B
Jesus you're the reason for a
```

Repeat Chorus
Repeat Bridge

Words and Music by: Andy Wilson, Crosskid Nation

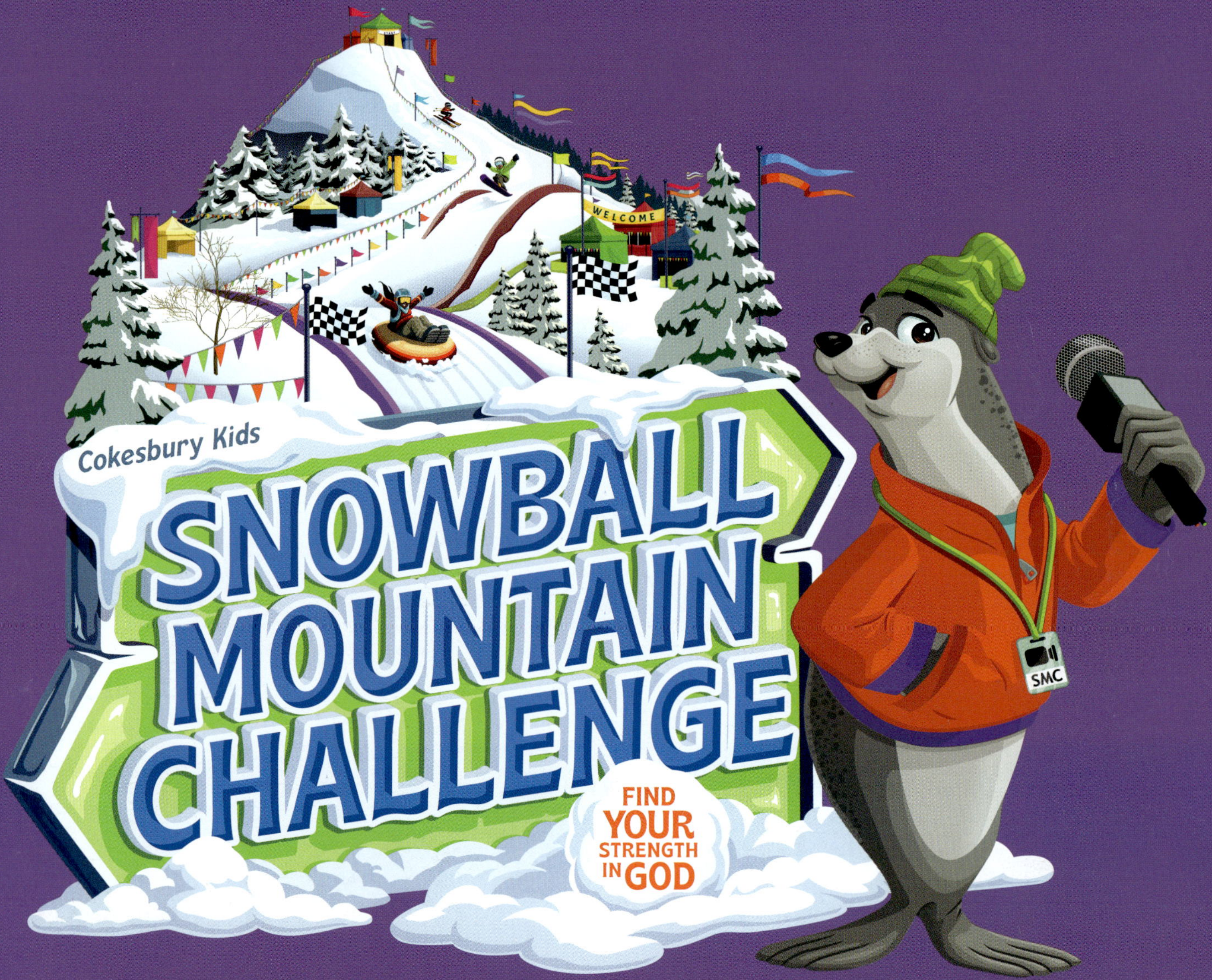

Cokesbury Kids

SNOWBALL MOUNTAIN CHALLENGE

FIND YOUR STRENGTH IN GOD

www.cokesburykids.com

RELIGION/Christian Education/Children & Youth

ISBN-13: 978-1-7910-3756-7